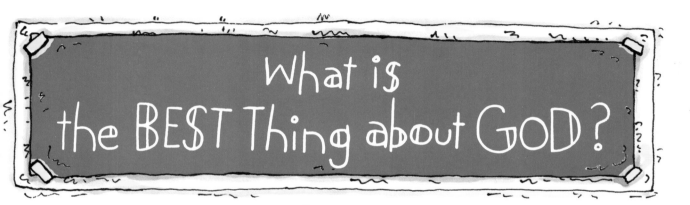

What is the BEST Thing about GOD?

This book is narrated by Christopher . . .

. . . but his voice is really the voice of Christine Harder Tangvald, author of more than 50 children's books. With her enthusiastic eye-level, heart-level style that kids really understand, Christine communicates to kids how much she cares. She's a mother and grandmother and has worked with children for more than 20 years. Christine and her husband, Roald, live in Spokane, Washington.

Dedicated to every parent, teacher, grandparent, and friend who communicates to a single child (even in a small way) the GIFT of LIFE — salvation through faith in our Lord and Savior, Jesus Christ. Such important work! Thank you, each one!
— C.H.T.

The Standard Publishing Company, Cincinnati, Ohio
A division of Standex International Corporation
Text © 1994 by Christine Harder Tangvald
Illustrations © 1994 by The Standard Publishing Company
All rights reserved.
Printed in the United States of America
01 00 99 98 97 96 95 94   5 4 3 2 1

Library of Congress Catalog Card Number 94-8031
ISBN 0-7847-0163-6
Cataloging-in-Publication data available

Edited by Diane Stortz
Designed by Coleen Davis

Scripture from the *International Children's Bible, New Century Version.*
© 1986, 1989 by Word Publishing, Dallas, Texas 75039.
Used by permission.

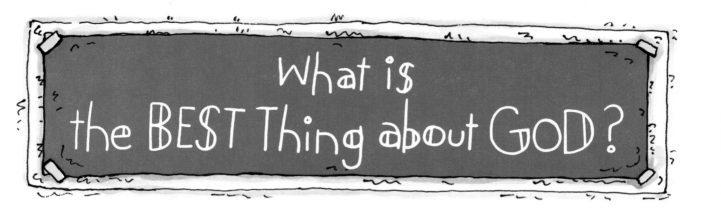

What is the BEST Thing about GOD?

written by Christine Harder Tangvald
illustrated by Kathy Couri

STANDARD
PUBLISHING
Cincinnati, Ohio

Oh! Hello there! How *are* you?
I am *so* glad to see you, because I need your help!

My name is Christopher,
and I have a problem, a big, *big* problem!
You see, I am making a book about the BEST thing about God.
But there are *so* many wonderful things about God
that it is *hard* to decide which is best.

Will you please
help me choose?
Will you please
help me finish
my *special* book?

You *will?* That's great!
First, let's go through
this book together.

(That will be fun!)

Then you can help me
choose which is the BEST
thing about God.
OK? Are you ready?
Here we *go!*

Do you think the BEST thing about God is his *power*?

God is *powerful*, you know.
He is strong and POWERFUL and *mighty*!

How powerful *is* God?
Oh, nobody knows.
But we do know that God is SO strong
and SO mighty and SO powerful
that he made the whole wide wonderful universe!

He did!

He made millions and *billions* and TRILLIONS
of stars
    and planets
        and comets

    that *whirl* and *twirl*
   and *zip* and *zoom* through space . . .
    . . . ALL OVER THE PLACE!

              Wow!

We don't know *how* God created so much space . . .
        . . . all over the place.

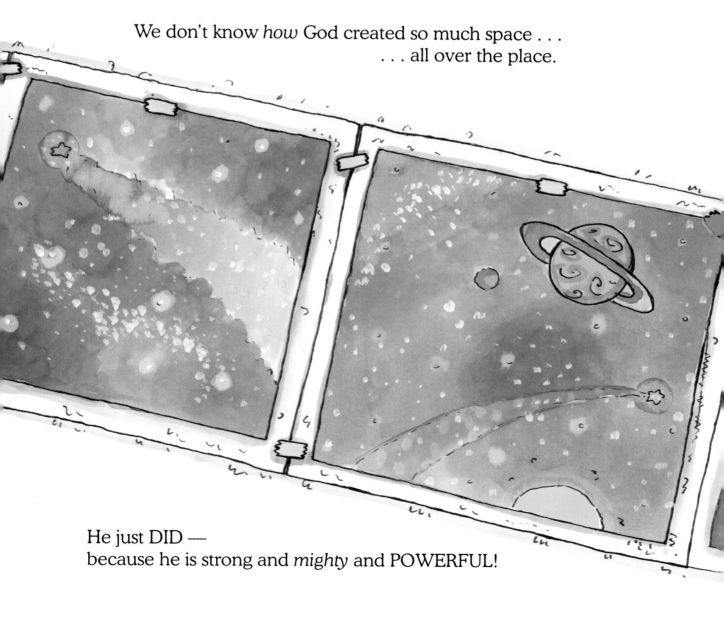

He just DID —
because he is strong and *mighty* and POWERFUL!

And God is SO powerful and SO mighty that he created our whole wide *wonderful* world.

He made it just for *us*. Isn't that GREAT?

First, he made
day and night . . .
with dark and light!

Then, he made high,
high mountains
with tall green trees.

He made *swishy-wishy* fish
in the deep blue seas.

He put *itsy-bitsy* spots on *itsy-bitsy* bugs!
He made sleek white swans —
and ugly old slugs!

And do you know what God did *then?*

Carefully, *carefully* . . . out of the dust of the earth,
    God made Adam — the very first man.
And carefully, *carefully,*
    God made Eve — to be Adam's wife.

And GOD breathed right into them . . . "Whooo — Whooooo" . . .
the breath of life!
Wow!

Oh, YES. Our God is strong and *mighty* and POWERFUL!
Maybe *that's* the BEST thing about God.

Put
your
photo
here.

But maybe the BEST thing about God
is that he made *you!*

He did, you know.
And even before you were born,
while you were just an itsy-bitsy,
teeny-*tiny* baby
still growing inside your mother,
God knew all about you!

He made you exactly
the way he wants
you to be —
exactly!

And I think
God did a VERY
good job.
Because I think you
are *wonderful.*
I think you
are TERRIFIC!

If you don't believe me,
just go look into the mirror — right now!

What do you see?
How tall are you?
What color are your eyes?
How many teeth do you have?
What color is your hair?
How many hairs do you have
on your head?
(Oh, don't count them now!
That would take too long.
But GUESS WHAT!
God knows *exactly*
how many hairs you have!)

He knows because
he made you.
He made you *special*
and different
from anybody
else in the *whole
wide world!*

I wonder
if that is the
BEST thing
about God —
that he made *you*
SO wonderful
and SO *special*.

Maybe the BEST thing about God is that he knows everything!

He does.
You see, God is smart — really, really smart!
In fact, God knows *everything* about EVERYTHING (and that is a *lot* of stuff to know!).

Not only that —
God *sees* everything and *hears* everything — ALL at the SAME TIME! Isn't that *amazing?*
And he *never* goes to sleep — *ever!*
I don't know how he does it.
He just does, because he is GOD!

So do you know what *that* means?
That means he is in charge!
God is in charge of *everything* . . . all the time. . . even right *now!*

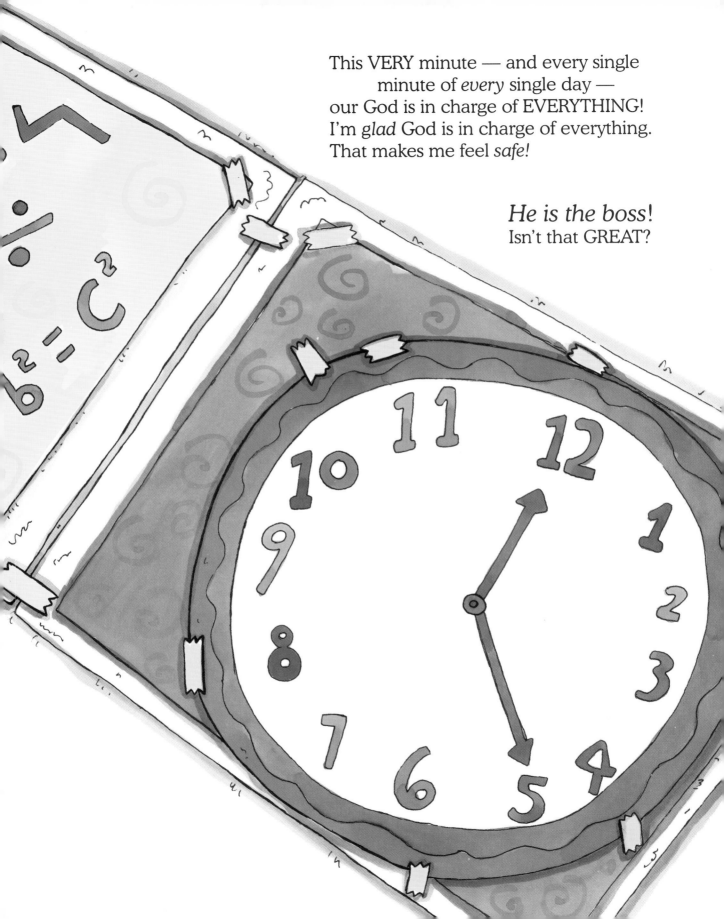

This VERY minute — and every single
minute of *every* single day —
our God is in charge of EVERYTHING!
I'm *glad* God is in charge of everything.
That makes me feel *safe!*

He is the boss!
Isn't that GREAT?

Well, if God is *in charge*,
and if he *knows* everything,

and *sees*
everything,

and *hears*
everything

do you think God can see
you and me right now?

Oh, YES. *Of course* he can!

God knows
and sees
everything
about you.

He knows if you
are **SAD,**

He loves you . . .
and likes you . . .
a LOT!

or **MAD,**

or **GLAD.**

HE knows . . .
and he cares!

Oh, YES.
God cares
because he
loves you.

Maybe *this* is
the BEST thing
about God —
that he *knows*
and he *cares*!

And because God cares,
     he does not want us to be lonely, or alone. Oh, NO!

So God sends his very own
     Holy Spirit right with me!

Everywhere I go,
God's Holy Spirit is right there with me.
If I go to the store,
     God's Holy Spirit goes with me.
If I go to church,
     God's Holy Spirit goes with me.

99¢

If I go to school . . .
     or to the doctor . . .

. . . or to Grandma's house . . .
or clear across the ocean —

or to the North Pole
or to the South Pole
or even to the moon! —

GOD'S HOLY SPIRIT IS WITH ME!

Isn't that *amazing?*

Maybe *that's* the BEST thing
about God — his wonderful Holy Spirit!

Do you ever talk to God?
I do. God likes it when we talk to him.

Talking to God is called *prayer*.
And it's SO easy!
You just say,

"Hi, God! It's me, _____ *(say your name)*."

And then you talk about anything you want to!
And you can talk to God anytime, from any place.

What are your favorite times and places to talk to God?

And *here* is the good part. God hears us!

I mean, you might think God would be *too busy*
to listen to us.

But he isn't. Oh, NO!
God is *never* too busy to listen to *your* prayer.

Because God thinks you are important —
— *very*, VERY important!

HEY! Do you have something you want to talk to God about —
right now?
Go ahead. I'll wait for you.

"Hi, God! It's me, _____ *(say your name)*.
Here is something I want to tell you, God.

_____

_____ ."

Amen! (That means, "the end.")

Maybe the BEST thing about God
is being able to talk to him — anytime,
anyplace, about anything!

But maybe the best thing about God
is his special book, the Bible.

Do you have a Bible in your house?

The Bible is full of wise,
wise words from God!
King Solomon said,
        "God's words are like
        a hidden treasure!"

Can *you* find
these treasures
in the Bible?

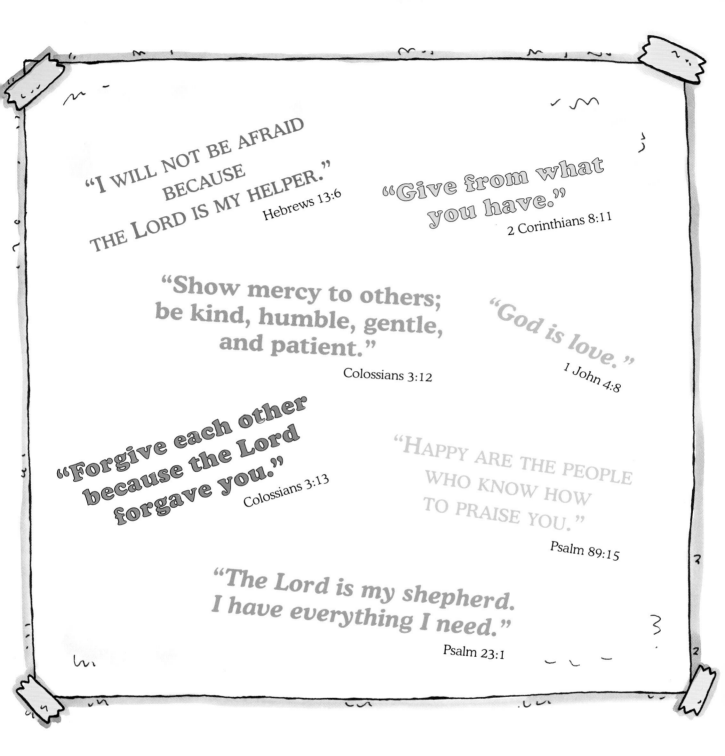

"I WILL NOT BE AFRAID BECAUSE THE LORD IS MY HELPER."
Hebrews 13:6

"Give from what you have."
2 Corinthians 8:11

"Show mercy to others; be kind, humble, gentle, and patient."
Colossians 3:12

"God is love."
1 John 4:8

"Forgive each other because the Lord forgave you."
Colossians 3:13

"HAPPY ARE THE PEOPLE WHO KNOW HOW TO PRAISE YOU."
Psalm 89:15

"The Lord is my shepherd. I have everything I need."
Psalm 23:1

Wow!
Do you know any other
of God's wise, wise words?

Have you ever been lost?
Have you ever gone the wrong way?

Oh, no. Oh, boy — it's *not* fun to be lost.
It's *not* fun to go the wrong way.
It is *scary!*

Well, God knows how to help us not get lost.
God knows how to help us go the right way in our life.

He does! God's wise, wise words in the Bible
help us choose the right way to go.

Yay! Hurray!
If we obey God's wise, *wise* words,
we can have lots and LOTS of fun
and be really, *really* happy!

I'm glad God knows the right way for you and me
to have a happy, happy heart!
Do you think this could be the BEST thing about God?

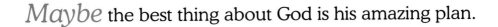

Maybe the best thing about God is his amazing plan.

You already know that God loves you, right?
He *does!* Lots and LOTS!

Well, God loves you SO much that he sent us
his own Son, Jesus,
to be *our* very own friend and Savior!
Can you believe that!

So, now, if we believe in Jesus (and I *do!*)
then God forgives all the bad things we think
and all the bad things we do.
All our sins are washed away —

Whoooosh! Swooosh!

They're GONE!

And someday, because of Jesus,
we can go to a special place called heaven,
and be there with Jesus forever
and *ever* and EVER!

Wow!

Isn't that a wonderful plan?
Isn't that an *amazing* plan?

Thank you, God.
Thank you for Jesus!

Maybe the very BEST thing about God is that . . .

God is GOD!

I mean, wouldn't it be terrible — *horrible* —
simply *awful* if there wasn't any God!

There wouldn't be any planets zooming through space!
There wouldn't be any whole wide wonderful world!
    — No fantastic, terrific you!
    — Nobody to pray to!
        — No Holy Spirit!
        — No Jesus!
    — No amazing plan for you and me!

There wouldn't be *anything!*

Nothing.   Nothing at all!   How AWFUL!

But, **God IS God!** and since he is . . .

there *are* planets whirling and twirling
through space . . .
Yay! Hooray!
And there *is* a whole wide wonderful world!
There *is* a terrific, fantastic you!
— We can talk to God!
— There is a wonderful Holy Spirit!
— Jesus is my friend and Savior!
— And there is an amazing plan . . .
. . . for you and me!
Yay! Hooray!

Oh, YES. I'm really, *really* glad that God is God,
aren't *you?*

Wow!
I think God is so WONDERFUL!
In fact, I love God *so much* that I want
to tell everyone else about him too!
I want to *shout,*

"Hey you guys!

I think God

is Super, terrific colossal, incredibly, fantastically wonderful!"

Don't *you?*

So, now you can see what a BIG problem I have.
    How can I *possibly* choose
    which is the BEST thing about God?
Will you please help me now?
Will you please help me choose?
    You will? Oh, *thank you!*

WELL,

what have you decided?

What did
you choose?

What do *you* think
is the BEST thing
about God?

Can you go back
and point to it with your finger?
　　　Or say it out loud, right now?

　　　Or write your answer here:
　　　I think the best thing about God is

_____

_____

_____ .

Wow!

That is a good thing about God
that you chose.
Thank you *so* much
for helping me finish
my book.

I couldn't have done
it without you!

$Well,$ this has been fun, hasn't it,
working on my book together?
>It is sad to say good-bye to you.
>I will miss you.

>Hey, I know what!
Maybe we can read through *this* book
together again sometime.
>I'd like that.
>I'd like it a *lot*.

Well, good-bye, my special friend!
And God bless you —
>today, tomorrow,
>and *always!*

Christopher